GANNO...

A TALE OF THREE T...

by Nina Murray

Published by The Braag
thebraag.co

The poems in this pamphlet were inspired by the life and writings of Larysa Kosach, the Ukrainian feminist thinker and poet known by her pen-name Lesya Ukrainka. Translating Ukrainka's plays, Cassandra first and foremost, became for me an experience of being possessed by Lesya's voice and imagination. The Tale of Three Thimbles is both a meditation on an iconised poet's life and my way to inhabit that feeling of being spoken-through.

Gannota

A word used for so long, most of the original meaning has worn off. A word worked over like vellum. Like a waxed thread. It means, a husband-less wife. A woman outside a man's custody. She presides. No longer, suppose, house-bound but surely still ground-tied. Land-locked. Already the mother to everything she'll ever mother. A creature who must be renamed in order to be defined.

#Larysanow

Somehow, Manitoba is always like this: rain hits me like I'm its gristmill and it's got a harvest to grind. Holds me open—I am the eye that steers tessellations. Sees spectres. The church a white smudge on the verdant horizon. Wind makes a bone-flute of the clapboard; rain fingernails under the paint—up and down the steeple. The well. I am a bolus on the tongue of the plains. Something about to be swallowed. My headlights blink. Out of the car. Into the house.

fog like oatmeal
superimposes states
each piece of a puzzle
spins four ways
the days are quantum

Gone Gannota. Gone Harpyna. Gone the first in the line of women to have carried the name Gannota, who while she was alive was much talked about.

In the spring, when the skin of the mountains began to sweat under the snow, and threads of water ran downhill, Harpyna could look into that water and tell where the pastures would be richest that year. She need only to place her hand on a newborn horse's withers to tell how many times his dam had fought off the wolves and how fast it would grow to be. She could smell a mitten off a man's hand and name all the women he had ever touched. She would never do this on a woman.

Lest you think her a heathen witch, know this: Harpyna was found in church every feast day and Sunday. She often cried there: said she mourned with the timbers for their lost kin that had been cut into the cross. Sometimes, she could stop a windmill.

Harpyna lived a long life but even her days could be counted. When she knew it was time, she called her one daughter, Oksana, into her room and bequeathed her a fine-tooled box of linden wood. Inside the box were three thimbles: one of iron, the other of silver, and the third one of gold.

What she told Oksana was meant for her alone and is not yours to know. The next day at dawn we saw Harpyna walk out of the village into the mountains. She looked neither right nor left, nor did she glance behind. When she was lost in the forest, a great clamour of rooks rose up from the trees, turned like a slow wheel of smoke in the sky, and ashed back down.

evensong
#archival

Ours is a meagre magic:
done stitch by stitch,
to be touched
only a few times a year.
On this night we can be certain
the mules and oxen will speak
in tongues that make sense
in the twisting worm-holes
of our human ears.
The ballads the herons sing,
the sagas the goats chant
are beyond us: too grand,
too finely spun. Still, give thanks:
Winter is a patient miller.
Straw into gold—the hours
when work makes mind invisible
ground into the dusting of daylight.
Darkness, unhurried, returns
man to that first primordial stall,
a naked thing dropped
into drifts of hay,
a nest warm and walled
with curtains of grainy breath.
Listen: mice congregate.

#martha #letters

jackdaws in the chimney
their beady clamouring
their petty imposition

how did it start
a solicitous peck
an invitation by head bob
to try this perch
to powder feathers
with soot

I too
am an impostor:
I impose on them
the clang of my poker
the quick fissile
flame on a bit of wool
smoke signals

they have gone quiet
do they trust me to be
the keeper of their safety
godmother to their
eventual brood

do they know
that I refuse?

#Larysanow

early on winter Sundays
this is what the chimney lays:
a feather, a spasmic yawn of the wind,
a date of birth singed
on a scalloped scrap of a letter,
cold pinches of ash that run like water,
fingerfuls, thumbprints.
this is what the laundry basket holds:
the brine of horseback thrill,
the dry skin of noons,
garden worms, strange appetites,
cratered, like moonscapes, caps of white mushrooms,
the skeletal indictment of dying mint.

this is how things come apart,
waves from the future
fail to cancel their counterparts
released from the past,
scrambling horoscopes and Tarot readings.

so when a telos finds a destination
it is an anchorage — slow,
snow flakes waltz on the windshield,
throw toe-loops on their diamond skates.

#thevoice

no language but naming
blood that inchoate swell
thump thump whoosh
squeeze of a larger heart
no there but here in and out
each sense a spot on an eel

#thevoice

where does the tongue start?
before the lap-clap
the lip-lap-clap that it does
on the walls of that dome
the smooth hard walls
the familiar reach-out-and-touch-them
walls

when does the bell begin?
what does it know, tongueless?
I hopscotch cobwebs sometimes
my laddered lily-pads
up to the bell to ask:
what is it like to be tongueless?
the bell-tower bones
wear threadbare slats
every March a pigeon
loses its grip
falls from the rafters
a pinwheel
a feathered propeller
wings useless
apaddle

when his heart clatters
against cage inside the bird
inside your mouth
does it feel like a kiss
or a throatful of dust?

11

Ironwater

Oksana gave her heart to a kind-eyed man who was a fine logger and deft with an axe—although that was nothing special in our parts. Marko was sharp as a tack, too, the quickest at learning his letters as a boy, with a memory like a steel trap (a tool he abhorred). When the call to war came again, Marko went into the Crown's army.

He came back years later, one-legged, with a veteran's pension, speaking in tongues. He told Oksana he would not begrudge her if she changed her mind, but if she still wished to marry him, he would never refuse her anything she asked for.

They had this talk at the hot spring her mother had found. Oksana there, limber in the steam on a cold day, wreathed in mosses and ferns, floated as light as a wisp of vapour herself. She saw him: a web of limbs and his cane strung between the trees. He trembled with love. The whole of him would have crumbled around her finger. She saw the fir needles slip off his hair, saw him as a thing of taut silk that shook itself free of any underserved burden, and nodded.

No one had seen her kiss the iron thimble on her finger and let it slip to the bottom of the pool. She came down the mountain with Marko, and they bought an inn at the closest railway station. Soon after, word spread that the hot spring could treat many ills. It made brittle bones grow tough as the spidersilk.

Sofia, once she read "of forms transformed to bodies new and strange," split her thimble, the silver one, into pieces. The bigger one was melted down and ultimately paid for her passage across the Atlantic. She had the rest fashioned into a set of needles. She sewed chickens shut and sometimes wounds, worked splinters loose from under nails and skewered ticks. The bigger one was named her "Gypsy" needle, Sofia herself dark-haired and out of the mountain country, alien enough to the lowland Mudrows and Melaniks who sailed on that ship, a shard of something that loomed somewhere behind them all, a flinty fulcrum.

Chew up a bite of bread, roll it, hold it under the petal of a baby's ear-lobe, the needle a quick blood draw. The daughter's blood, the mother's bread, Sofia's one piece of silver. Year after year until it's lore. Red thread, then, through the puncture, wool to take the place of blood. A trade.

Sofia had sons.

The line meanders, skips. The gold thimble passed on to Larysa, Sofia's niece.

Larysa is born a poet. When Martha, her sister, is born, calls her birdie. Herself a goshawk, a sharp-breasted, ferocious thing. Plays at Mycenae, Aeschylus reworked for two girls and a reddish quilt.

Collects wedding songs.

When Martha marries a priest, follows them to Manitoba, oecumene's edge. The new land defies her, belongs to those by whom it is known. Categories slip. The church a shore where shipwrecks are preemptive—before crossing West people leave: a piano, a sewing machine, a home-made model of human brain made with wire and ribbon.

Another war in the old world, a hope for statehood. Volunteers rally. The sisters melt the gold thimble—the time for caution feels gone. They spin the gold into thread then sit up nights to embroider a banner. The work is surgical, stitches hold together layers of canvas (tobacco sacks—the smell lingers like home), velvet trim.

The banner is the only thing that comes back. The dark futile mass of it stands in the corner, a coffin lid.

a glossa for Wallace Stevens

Troops cross the road and beyond the pines
drop whole into the bristly lap of gorse.
Marines pull 'round the cloak of camouflage,
Spy this: The mules that angels ride
come slowly down.

What else to watch on these fog-curried hills?
Our squadroned intuition is of shedding:
the sand sloughs off its heavy pebbled skin,
pine needles, cones—it dreams, like us, of blazing
passes from beyond the sun.
We dig. Stones bulge like skulls.
Chew up our spades in gears of unmaking.
The gravel's toothy as a bulldozed pit.
Against the steel, descensions
of its tinkling bells arrive.

Into the pines, dear old ghosts recede.
We tether tents, ourselves,
these muleteers are dainty on their feet.

#Larysathen

Dear Cassandra —

I want to believe you survived. Wounded, perhaps, or left for dead, or somehow just overlooked.

Unseen, this one time. I hope you made it out of Agamemnon's palace—once the moist crack of his skull, the convulsed splashing, slipping, thrashing, the seconds—or minutes—it took to turn that man into a corpse—unleashed pandemonium. I hope you pulled your cloak low over your face, grabbed a handful of yet-to-be-spun wool abandoned by another panicked woman and started walking.

I hope no one asked you any questions.

I hope you then sat down to spin—yourself your own Moira—settling your nerves with the rhythmic motion of your fingers. You refused to see. If you did not ask yourself what was next, you did not have to answer.

Perhaps a dog came by—one of those lop-eared, curly-tailed animals on haunches like poured bronze that can do any kind of work. I see him plop down in the road dust at your feet, grateful for company.

Eventually you stood, and the dog stood, and you followed him to a shadowed spring, mud around it cratered by goats' hooves. I don't know if you found a new family. I hope you didn't. I hope you got to claim those woods as a sanctuary. I hope you spun the wool and strung lengths of it around the trunk of an old linden, beribboned with seed-pods. Sometimes, if you found a bird skull left behind by a fox (or the dog, who stayed with you, making you wonder if perhaps he was another survivor of murderous but not entirely effective magic, someone the gods had transformed and then forgot about) you would pick it up and hang it on your linden belt, strung through the eye-socket.

You would listen to the delicate, husky knock of the bird bones against the skin of the tree as you sat with your back pressed against the trunk and sensed the ferocious uprush of life from root to crown. You would feel the quivering echo of it in your own spine and have no need to speak anything at all.

#Larysathen

I saw the shimmer of the meadowlark and heard
the whisper of dry rush along the road
a prayer for the health, perhaps, of newt and toad,
a litany of snows come and gone,
the ploughed-up fossils and the muddy pun
of hoofprints on the bridle path. The Gothic steeple
a finger raised to shush the clouds, a beacon
for the ghosts of shepherds and their phantom herds.

Time folds before me, compresses into flint.
A thousand years while the wild plum and the willow
blossom along the edges of the field. My hair billows,
I take the trail to where I haven't been,
rhyme comes to claim its ostentatious glint.
I look for Roman coins; find rabbit bones, gnawed clean.

#archival #news

On the 150th anniversary of the famous poet, Larysa Gannota's, birth, her body is exhumed from its grave in what is today a suburb of Winnipeg to be repatriated to her birthplace, Kolomyia. Playing undertaker, the government undertakes the work of rediscovery, recovery, mourning. Autopsy of the author. In her work, autotelic. Poet: an apiary rhymed into ossuary. Decay arrested. Intrusion authorised. The finds: the poet, legendarily virginal, had been pregnant, once. The gold tooth in her mouth is hollow, had held cyanide. Bones honeycombed by dis-ease. Nothing broken. Exemplary posture. A loop of gold thread wound in her womb, a laurel.

#thevoice

let it be spring. daffodils piebald the green. trees mere lacework, easy to see. mud. all details are not important. what is desperation? two women with bloodied hands. (what is a clove? that which cleaves). the cyclops' eye cycles, eulogising. blood on the floor. blood between Larysa's legs. rags. a quilt pulled apart. she opens her fist: a spool of gold thread. no one will miss a loop. make a slip-knot. you can do it, birdie. they scrub everything later. gravity guttered. the gutter an oyster, a maw for details. the mire of it. cold water, chapped hands, bury the rags. keep clean. make clean. stand up straight, the shock of it. water is barrel rain, trapped snow. pretend. pretend.

#Larysanow

Under the gloaming sky the grasses grow light,
Anticipating moonlight, ribbon-like.
There's consolation in the falling dusk.

I have no thoughts, I stare into the bright
glass of the kitchen doors. I hold a knife,
while outside, the grasses grow light.

A premonition hovers, strong as musk:
Our plans are mere fingers in the dyke.
There's consolation in the falling dusk.

Why cast yourself a hero, the Shining Knight
when rain nests in the dahlias, bird-like—
all objects come to rest, try as we might.

Drunk on the porter of the night, my hopes unmask
and stand for what they are — a mist of Brownian mites.
There's consolation in the falling dusk.

Your mind, if armoured with a pair of tusks,
would separate the woof of time — a single strike
to catch electrons from a future light.
There's consolation in the falling dusk.

#Larysanow

the blood matches

the body
the banner

22

#thevoice

one is a reaper
two is a cry
three is coven
more is a tribe

one is a spinner
two is a plan
three is a prophecy
more is a clan

one is a refugee
two is a home
three plant an orchard
among the gravestones

Notes and Acknowlegements

This book would not be possible without the kind and marvellous touch of Dr. Alexa Doran.
'Early on winter Sundays' is inspired by 'Three Poems' by Hannah Sullivan.

Illustration on page 2 from 'Horizontal Panel with Three Thimble Designs and Two Medallions' from The Elisha Whittelsey Collection, The Elisha Whittelsey Fund, 1951.

Cover design by Nathaniel Spain. Cover detail: Ukrainian shirt fragment, Brooklyn Museum Costume Collection at The Metropolitan Museum of Art.

Nina Murray is a Ukrainian-American poet and translator. She is the author of the poetry collections *Glapthorn Circular* (LiveCanon Poetry, 2023) and *Alcestis in the Underworld* (Circling Rivers Press, 2019) as well as several chapbooks. Her award-winning translations include Oksana Zabuzhko's *Museum of Abandoned Secrets* (Amazon Crossing), and Oksana Lutsyshyna's *Ivan and Phoebe* (Deep Vellum). Her translation of Lesia Ukrainka's *Cassandra* was performed at the Omnibus Theatre in London in 2022 and toured to Cambridge and Oxford in 2023. Nina grew up in Lviv and lives, for the moment, in Cambridgeshire.

This manuscript was edited and typeset by Kym Deyn for The Braag. The Braag CIC is a publisher of speculative fiction and poetry chapbooks and of the quarterly micro-journal Carmen et Error. It supports writers in the north east of England through publications and events, and works with writers across the globe. It focuses on weird, wild fiction and poetry and produces beautiful things on a small scale. More information can be found at thebraag.co.